CARTOON MOUSE (Squeaky Mouse)

INDIAN MOUSE (Mouse-Chief)

Molto moderato

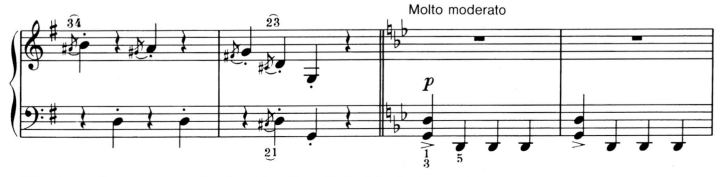

*Play the small notes very rapidly, almost together with the following large note.

4

RUSSIAN MOUSE (Mousse Russe)

Much slower

VIENNESE MOUSE (Strauss Mouse)

Tempo di Valse

BUSY MOUSE (House Mouse)

Allegro molto

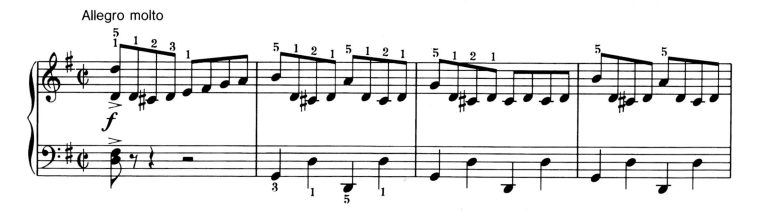

LONG-HAIRED MOUSE (Eine Kleine Nachtmouse*)

*A Little Night-Mouse, by Mouzart.

Alfred's Basic Piano Library

Willard A. Palmer • Morton Manus • Amanda Vick Lethco

A PIANO COURSE
FOR BEGINNERS OF ALL AGES

Alfred's Basic Piano Library offers nine perfectly graded beginning series which are designed to prepare students of all ages for a successful musical learning experience. With the exception of **Alfred's Basic Adult Piano Course,** which is complete in itself, all of the beginning series are interchangeable at several levels (see arrows below), and lead into the main **Alfred's Basic** course, which is complete through Level 6 (seven levels all together). This course, then, is the most flexible of any method in allowing the teacher to personally design a specific curriculum according to the age and needs of each individual student. On completion, the student is ready to begin playing the great piano masterworks.

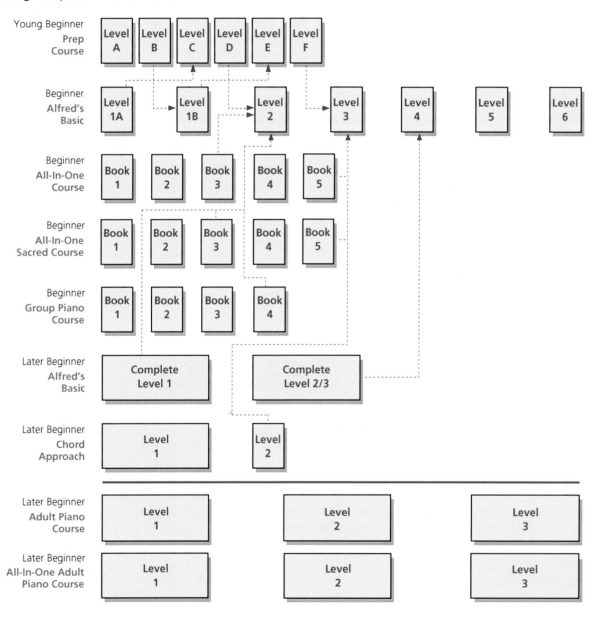

Alfred Publishing Co., Inc.
16320 Roscoe Blvd., Suite 100
P.O. Box 10003
Van Nuys, CA 91410-0003
alfred.com

3145

$4.

ISBN 0-7390-1525-7